21 LESSONS OF TECH INTEGRATION COACHING

MARTINE BROWN

Copyright © 2019 by Martine Brown

All rights reserved.

No part of this book may be reproduced in any form or by any electronic or mechanical means, including information storage and retrieval systems, without written permission from the author, except for the use of brief quotations in a book review.

(*) Denotes that digital content is available online at www. martinembrown.com password: 21lessons

ISBN: 978-1-970133-35-6

CONTENTS

Foreword	vii
Introduction	ix
1. Lessons 1-3: The Shift	1
2. Lessons 4-6: Anatomy of a Coach	11
3. Lessons 7-9: Coaching and Growing Teacher Leaders	23
4. Lessons 10-12: Learning From the PLN	35
5. Lesson 13-15: Back to the Not-So-Basics of School	45
6. Lesson 16-18: Howdy Partner! Instructional Coaching Partnerships	55
7. Lesson 19-21: Not Another PD?	61
8. Conclusion	71
Acknowledgments	79
References	81

APPENDIX

Sample Action Plan	87
Websites	89
Coaches to Follow	91
Other EduMatch Titles	93

For my parents,

Jennifer and Donald,

for their dreams set me free...

FOREWORD

I am overjoyed to write this foreword. Not only has Martine Brown been a thinking partner and fellow edtech coaching friend of mine for many years, but I wholeheartedly believe in the power of teacher support and professional development through coaching and support. Over the past few years, I have learned from the support Martine provides teachers and students, and I have also benefited from her support, resources, and passion for digital teaching and learning.

Learning is a reciprocal journey of give and take. While teachers are charged with helping students learn and grow, they need someone who will enable them to do the same. When I first became a teacher, I was surrounded by my former teachers. People who spent years pouring into me as I sat in their classrooms as a student. They were eager to take me under their wings, pick me up when I was down, and provide honest, open feedback when I needed it most. Their assistance during my first few years proved to be instrumental in my professional growth and development. There were so many things I didn't know, and my informal teachers made it easy for me to come to them with questions and concerns. They always had an open door for me to walk through as a new teacher in need of support.

The same is true for educators who are gifted the opportunity to teach with technology. Martine has a passion for solid content and pedagogy. Coupled with her passion for digital teaching and learning, she has written a book to help coaches to sharpen their skills to provide the best support for those they serve. Who's going to coach the coach? Martine is here to help us all. This book will give practical lessons to help you grow as an instructional leader and help you to build capacity in others.

I hope this book will become a guide for those looking for practical strategies to implement and lessons from which they can grow.

— Knikole Taylor

INTRODUCTION

Me, Instructional Leader? I'm A Classroom Lifer.

When I consider the path that has led me to write this book, I have to be honest about my journey. I didn't know I was going to be an instructional coach. What I mean by that is, this idea of supporting teachers regardless of their content was foreign to me. I was a self-proclaimed "lifer." Much like my mentors, I felt that my role in education would lead to a lifetime of helping teens succeed as an English, Speech, and College Readiness teacher. I have always had a love for children, and working with teenagers allowed me to help students actualize their dreams as they prepared to transition into colleges, universities, certification programs, and trade schools. This was, and still is, my passion. I knew I would only get to see the effects of my impact occasionally happen, which ignited my fire to fight every year to help the next group of students craft better reading and writing strategies to aid them as they navigate life. Yet, I found something new in coaching, and the movement from building student capacity to nurturing adult learners has helped me reshape my purpose while remaining authentic to my vision for fostering positive change in the lives of those around me.

So, the question then becomes, how did I become an instructional coach?

At the request of my department head, I joined my district's technology leadership program. We met a couple of times throughout the year, and I quickly realized that these experiences were helping to streamline my classroom practice. I was leaving each session more empowered with strategies and tools to enhance the lessons I taught. As it related to tech integration, I had more purpose around my rationale for integrating technology. For the first time in my career, I had the tools to reflect on my practices and how my teaching frameworks could improve my productivity, instruction, feedback, and classroom management. Furthermore, my students were becoming advocates for their learning and noted that my room was a place that they could learn and communicate in new ways that helped them to flourish with the content and beyond.

As an instructional technology representative on campus, I was asked to provide professional development to explore digital tools for the classroom. This was a new role for me, as I had limited experience (which was more like slim to none) with providing professional development. I knew early on, however, that I wanted to shy away from the humdrum, lecture-style sessions that I had received as an adult learner. These sessions had extinguished all hope I had of getting the kind of learning I needed to improve as an educator. The technology training and development I had been receiving was different. It sparked an understanding that professional development required the same energy, design elements, and connectedness that was necessary to foster engagement with students.

During the session I led on digital competencies, I had a teacher who said to me how nervous she was and how little she knew about the mobile devices that would soon be in the hands of all our students. Her sentiment reverberated around the room, and I realized that integrating technology into the learning environment was indeed a challenge for many. I remember looking at her wholeheartedly and share with her that none of us is alone in this change. You have me to lean on. This is the moment that I became an instructional coach. I was determined to help other educators see and fulfill their own potential. Much like teaching, somewhere along the way, a new calling in my life was born. I could no longer remain in my classroom day in and day out when I knew that my colleagues needed support as they learned to navigate new tools and pedagogies that would transform their practices and enhance the academic lives of the students. This path has helped me learn that every teacher deserves regular, individualized support in their professional growth.

Furthermore, the focus must be founded on creating personalized coaching structures that put student and teacher needs at the center of the work. It is from this place that I share 21 lessons that I have learned as an instructional coach. From these experiences, I will share strategies and techniques that help to support educators in designing instructional experiences that cultivate future-ready schools.

1

LESSONS 1-3: THE SHIFT

> *Everybody ain't gonna use your brain, honey."*

—Maxine Richardson Spates, My MiMi (My Grandmother)

Lesson 1: Expand Your Reach

What Is Your Why?

Transitioning from the classroom into an instructional coaching role requires a close examination of one's philosophical beliefs of their work as an educator. Much of my identity as an educator is closely aligned to the passion I have for teaching and learning. As I considered my own passions, I posed the following questions: How do I share this love for education with my colleagues and other professionals? How do I redefine my path as an educator? From a foundational standpoint, I knew that I wanted to make a difference. This concept is at the core of my educational philosophy. Here is how I did the math. If I taught 140-160 students each year, that meant I had the potential to impact learning for that group of students. In this new role, if I was able to influence a professional learning community or grade level team, then that influence has expanded exponentially. My impact grew to hundreds, possibly thousands of students, and I soon realized that I was able to continue my work without moving too far away from my original purpose.

The year before I began my work as an instructional coach, I was implementing a new strategy I had learned in training. In talking with one of my colleagues, she decided that she wanted to try the same technique in her lessons. That afternoon, we discussed her perceptions regarding the lesson as well as her thoughts about how she would use the strategy in the future. Little did I know, I was implementing a coaching cycle in its most organic nature. I followed the process of collaborating, planning, observing, and participating in reflective structures that supported the professional growth of the educator while also fostering instructional design. Expanding my reach had commenced, and even though I wasn't able to actualize its impact at the time, the experience has stayed with me. It reminds me to enter each educational partnership with a spirit of giving and growing together.

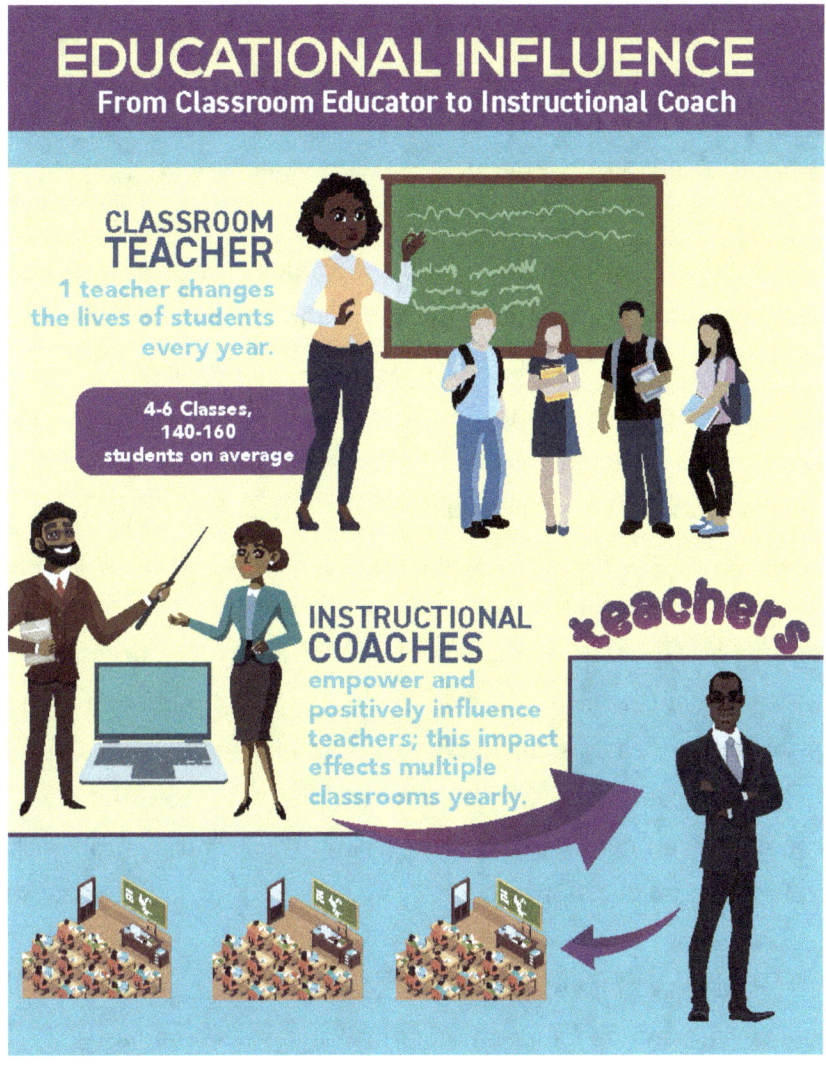

To be honest, everyone is not meant to be an instructional coach. I once met a phenomenal educator who had demonstrated a passion for the work she did with her students. Her plans, lessons, and activities were an administrator's dream come true. Her classes had used the problem-based learning model to develop numerous projects that had real-world implications. She and her students met with industry professionals to plan out their ideas, and even built an online store to market and sell their products. I secretly wished there was a way to recruit her the 3,000 miles it would take for her to serve on my campus. As we talked, she mentioned that she had taken a position as an instructional coach for one year. But she found the challenges of coaching and influencing others to be an insurmountable task- in which she found that her colleagues struggled with change, openness, and a desire to collaborate with others outside of traditional teaching teams. The following year she returned to the classroom, the place where she knew she could make a difference. To be frank, I actually believe that with more time, this educator would have been a phenomenal instructional coach. However, I think reflection and self-analysis are inherently necessary for deciding if instructional coaching is right for you. It doesn't matter what the principal, colleagues, or even friends think about your ability. Self-examination is at the core of transitioning from the classroom. As you consider or even prepare to take on this role, ask yourself these questions:

1. Who have I helped as it relates to adult learning? In what ways do I support other teachers on the campus instructionally?
2. What professional standards do I use to guide my own professional growth?
3. How do I plan for my own professional growth?
4. Do I provide professional development locally, regionally, nationally? If so, why? If not, what is holding me back?

5. How have I engaged in district/school programs and initiatives to help connect classroom practice with the overall vision?
6. Outside of teaching, what projects have I managed to support a large team of people or the school?
7. What are the driving factors of considering this role? Will these motivators keep me on track with my professional goals/mission?
8. What research have I examined as it relates to instructional coaching? How has that research helped me understand the role? (possibly reading this book, and for that, I say Thank YOU.)

Asking reflective questions like these will help you shape your why for being an instructional coach. For me, I realized early on that I this kind of work gave me joy, and when I considered many of these same questions, I knew that it was work that would continue to ignite my passion in education.

Lesson 2: "When I was in the Classroom" Myth

I have always loved working with teachers and colleagues. Whether they be mentors, professional learning community (PLC) members, or grade level partners, these colleagues help me shape my lessons and provide me a collaborative space to grow. As an instructional coach, especially one that doesn't teach students day in and day out, you must be mindful of how your perception of instruction impacts the development of teacher/coach partnerships. My grandmother used to say, "Everybody ain't gonna use your brain, honey." Being the wise woman that she was, my grandmother had a clear understanding of the power of perception. Just because you have a specific view of what teaching, learning, and growth looks like, does not mean that your perceptions apply to everyone. As the coach, your opinions are singular, and the only time a coach can ensure success within their partnerships is when they avoid language that assumes that we know the minds of our colleagues. That being said, I quickly realized that using the term, "when I was in the classroom," or "when I taught that subject" are caustic phrases. These one-liners imply that as a coach, your self-nominated, personal testimonies of success in the classroom are not only more valuable than the teacher's thoughts and ideas, but they destroy coaching relationships and the potential for developing partnerships to enhance instruction.

Lesson 3: Become a Partner and Researcher

As instructional coaches, we must remember to never be far removed from the classroom. Now more than ever, a teacher's day is spent juggling various hall duties, special education meetings, professional learning community meetings, lesson planning, parent conferences, and phone calls. If they are lucky, teachers get some instructional time that is meaningful for students squeezed into an extremely busy workday. With this in mind, the most precious commodity a teacher can gain is time. An instructional coach represents "time on its feet." We fill the gap between a teacher having an excellent idea and the time needed to research and fully execute the plan for that idea.

Newsletter No-No

Throughout my first year as an instructional coach, I spent a lot of time researching and creating newsletters. I did a combination of weekly video reports, email reports, and newsletters. My designs and ideas were succinct and based on the campus and district initiatives featuring tools, resources, and programs offered during the month. Over time, I realized that no one was reading them. I may have had a few people take a look at them. At one point, I even broke them down and personalized them to fit each of the departments I served, but to no avail. I got the feeling that they were ending up in the pile of unread emails or even worse, the trash bin. As I reflected on why this was happening, the answer was simple. Folks did not have time, and frankly, I was essentially spamming my colleagues. It had nothing to do with the content, and everything to do with the delivery of content. I wasn't the partner that I had set out to become when I took on the position, and all the materials I created -well, they weren't helping me be the agent of change that I sought out to be.

Building Partnerships

The next year, I decided to discontinue my newsletters and focus on building relationships. That is when I saw a huge change in how I was able to empower teachers. I worked with a team of teachers, and we met monthly for training. It was there that I was able to explore what teachers actually needed instead of what I thought they needed. Based on what they learned during training, they decided how they wanted to implement the ideas in their classrooms. I supported this process through researching tools, strategies to consider, or creating content such as student tutorials or overview videos. The power behind building these types of partnerships is that I was able to be the *time* that the teacher needed to develop learning experiences that often went by the wayside. As I became more confident in my ability to work with teacher leaders, I began to seek out more partnerships with campus librarians and assistant principals to forge new teacher relationships that would help me remain arm-in-arm with classroom educators. This way together, we could enhance instruction and increase student engagement in authentic learning.

Questions to Consider

At the end of each chapter, you will notice a section called "Questions to Consider" I encourage you to use the reflective questions to make connections to your current practice.

Questions to Consider from Chapter 1:

What is your *why* in working as an instructional coach? How will you use that purpose to drive change in schools?

How can you support teachers by leveraging their experiences in the classroom, while decentering from your own?

What considerations should you make when developing newsletters or deliverables to your staff? How will measure the effectiveness of the content that is being sent to your staff?

Reflective notes:

2

LESSONS 4-6: ANATOMY OF A COACH

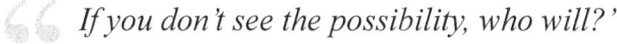 *If you don't see the possibility, who will?"*

—Kathy Kee, *Results Coaching Global*

Lesson 4: A Vision of Hope

I think the greatest challenge of instructional coaching is that it requires one to have an undeniable and authentic sense of hope every day. As an instructional coach, I am working on a campus to convince teachers and leadership to change their practices. As a novice teacher, one leans on what they experienced as a student. For veterans, arriving at a place that feels comfortable takes time, but it can also create professional stagnancy. This always takes me back to my third and fourth year of teaching. By that point I had a rhythm, my lessons and resources had been set for almost three years, and for the most part, I knew how I wanted to craft a lesson — where it would go and how students would generally respond. By year eight, there was not much anyone could do to change my patterns. I didn't mind adding and modifying bits and pieces, but building brand new lessons without cause (not district-mandated, not driven by PLCs) wasn't likely to happen. At the time, I lacked inspiration and didn't really have a reason to change.

Instructional Coaches: A Key Factor in Improving Pedagogical Practice

This sentiment above is not unusual, and as more instructional coaches are embedded into K-12 schools, this knowledge is imperative to understand the power of hope in our practice. According to Matthew Kraft and David Blazar's 60-study research on the impact of instructional coaching, "instructional coaching improves both instructional practice and student achievement--more so than other professional development and school-based interventions" (Kraft & Blazar, 2018 in Will, 2019). Acclaimed research associate and Director of Instructional Coaching Institutes at the Kansas University Center for Research on Learning, Jim Knight explains to the School Superintendents Association (ASSA) that "by offering support, feedback, and intensive, individualized professional learning, coaching promises to be a better way to improve instruction in schools" (Knight, 2018).

I have to believe that each staff member comes with a unique story and that both their personal and professional journeys impact how they accept change in their daily work. Some will be ready, flexible, and prepared to work with you. For others, it may be difficult to tap into the educator's instructional practices because as the instructional coach, you represent all of the changes that they don't want to happen. Moreover, the idea of acknowledging potential changes makes them uncomfortable.

This is why seeing what is possible in every staff member is so critical to championing change in schools. This level of personalized professional growth can incite systemic and complete change in how an educator facilitates learning in their classroom. Moving into each coaching connection with unabashed hope creates three favorable results from your staff: they trust you, they value your insights, and you can create the *snowball* effect. This shift in your thinking allows you to grow even the smallest success within your coaching experiences.

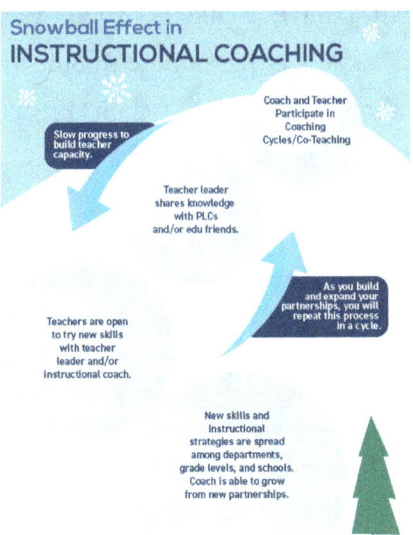

A Word About the Snowball Effect

Much like a snowball rolling down a hill, influencing change on campus has a lot to do with starting small. I tend to seek out teachers who are open to change and who are willing to work with me. These are individuals who are excited about instruction, or maybe they have taken on a new course and need support with building the curriculum. They might be a new teacher or a veteran. I also tap into school leaders as they can also be a source of inspiration and a key stakeholder (but I will talk about leadership a bit later). I look for ways to uplift the great work they are doing on campus through email, verbal encouragement, and shoutouts via social media. I also look for ways to support teachers instructionally, within workflows, or to improve daily productivity. What I have found is when we learn something together that the teacher is passionate about, the first thing that happens is that they share it with their Professional Learning Communities, or PLC teams.

Many times, I find out later that they teach what they have learned to their team. Finding the right teacher to work with is the key to growing the learning of the whole team, or essentially snowballing the learning. When this happens, it is imperative to double back, uplift, and encourage the whole team. From time to time, I will even drop a card in the educator's mailbox, cc the principal on an email about their work as a team, stop by a meeting, or observe a class to increase positive teacher attitudes about the changes that have organically happened on the team. I also have to add that this snowball effect often takes time. Think of a really really slow-moving mound of snow that gradually picks up speed, but eventually, its impact is massive! This practice supports redesigned lessons and improved teacher productivity.

Lesson 5: EARS Wide Open

As a teacher, my ear for listening needed a ton of work. I say this a bit tongue-in-cheek, but what I mean is that as a classroom teacher, I really didn't *have* to listen. I was the teacher; my students' top priority was to listen to instructions, pay attention during lectures or activities, and follow the directions. Then I reviewed their understanding in the form of an assessment and provided feedback. I think of all the skills needed to be an instructional coach; this one is vital. What I am referring to is active, focused listening in a way that is both personalized and unique within each interaction you have.

A few years back, I remember holding a focus group and walked away with a huge lesson regarding listening. During the focus group, the members were attentive and provided feedback that served as a great resource for our leadership. Our agenda was to review the 10 questions and use them as a catalyst for discussion.

The purpose of this focus group was to gather information regarding the assessment of professional development and its impact on teacher professional growth, classroom instruction, and student achievement. Several questions garnered strong responses that had the potential to improve campus culture and support building relationships. The first question asked specifically about what goals teachers had for professional development. As I listened, I realized that no one really had any specific goals or their responses varied, but in general, their answers did not align with the feedback that I had hoped to receive. From this, I realized that this may be an unspoken need or that I needed to clarify the question to the group. The book *Results Coaching Next Steps* (Kee, Anderson, Dearing, & Shuster, 2017, p. 58) notes that "committed listening lays the path for responses and solutions." The authors further this idea with the concept of "listening for the wants, emotions, passion, and potential of your respondents" (Kee et al., 2017, p. 59). As an instructional coach, using listening strategies during focus groups or anytime you are working with others supports your ability to guide solutions that build teacher capacity and ownership. From a leadership perspective, this experience really helped me understand the power of listening and how that process helps influence change and spark ideas.

Lesson 6: Heart for Coaching—Language

In college, word counts were one of the most important parts of writing a paper. Staying within the appropriate word count was essential to keeping within some of the most basic instructions given by a professor. The same is true for instructional coaching. Every. Word. Counts. In this sense, the words you choose to use or omit can make the difference between developing solid coaching cycles or disjointed coaching processes. In Sandra Trach's Article, Inspired Instructional Coaching (2014), she describes instructional coaching as a,

> ...relationship [that] is both transformational and reciprocal, benefiting the coach and teacher alike. Instructional coaching is an authentic instructional relationship, where each partner is professionally transformed and ultimately renewed each time they engage with one another about teaching and learning."

If one's ability to see the good in others is the foundation of building strong coaching experiences, then the pillars of coaching are fostered through developing your language. Because having transformative coaching partnerships are the foundation of the work, one of the first steps you should make is to redesign your language. Reflect on the language you used as a classroom teacher. Are you assertive and firm? Or do you tend to be more soft-spoken? In what ways does sarcasm or humor play a role in how you communicate? All of these questions should be explored. As an instructional coach, this information is key because you may need to adjust from one coaching experience to the next to build successful coaching relationships. Now, this is not to say that you should change yourself to meet the needs of your staff. Thinking and reflecting on your pre-coaching language has everything to do with honing your best self. When you think about the most successful students in your class, what language did you use to reach them? How did you alter your language to meet the needs of everyone while remaining your authentic self? What will you need to leave behind? The answers to these questions are unique to each of us and are key to establishing how we each connect with others during each coaching interaction.

Growing your Instructional Coaching Expertise

Here is a list of resources to help guide you on your journey of developing your instructional coaching practices. These are some of my go-to resources as I lean on them for ongoing growth.

The Coaching Habit. Ask More, Say Less and Change the Way

You Lead Forever by Michael Bungay Stanier (2016): This book has an awesome approach to begin your journey into coaching. The strategies are practical and can be implemented immediately with key questions to guide your coaching proficiency.

The Art of Coaching: Effective Strategies for School Transformation by Elena Aguilar (2013): This is an excellent resource for understanding your role as a coach. I specifically like the way she incorporates strategies that correlate with developing coaching conversations.

Everyday Instructional Coaching by Nathan Lang-Raad (2018): This text is not only practical, but provides a principles-based approach to engaging in habits that foster strong coaching experiences.

RESULTS Coaching: The New Essential for School Leaders (Kee, Anderson, Dearning, Harris & Shuster, 2010): A complete guide to fostering skills for coaching. What I specifically like about this book is that it provides sentence stems and examples of dialogue to promote language that helps coaches craft empowering coaching cycles.

RESULTS Coaching Next Steps: Leading for Growth and Change (Kee, Anderson, Dearning, Harris, & Shuster, 2017): This book offers a great combination of instructional coaching practices with supervisory roles in the professional setting.

Impact Cycle by Jim Knight (2018): This book provides an in-depth view of understanding how to systematically engage in coaching cycles. There are videos nested throughout the book to aid one in developing strong coaching skills.

> **Questions to Consider from Chapter 2:**
>
> Reflect on the Coaches' Anatomy: what are some aspects of the coaches' anatomy that you excel in? Where can you improve?
>
> In what ways will you structure your language?
>
> How will you instill a sense of hope into your practice each and every day?

Reflective notes:

3

LESSONS 7-9: COACHING AND GROWING TEACHER LEADERS

> *Coming together is a beginning, staying together is progress, and working together is success."* – Henry Ford

Lesson 7: Coming Together—Developing your Team

When building the capacity for change in school, developing a leadership team was an essential part of my growth as an instructional coach. This team of teacher leaders are essentially ambassadors for instructional design and digital integration. Ideas that were loved and shared by the group were disseminated to teacher friends and during PLC meetings. Teachers who learned or heard ideas from a team member would email with more questions or schedule a coaching session with me. One year, I had one of my team members stop by my office with a teacher who was reluctant to use a tool in her classes. I shared the benefits and options, but it was the confidence of my team member- their belief that the activity and the tool would be successful for learning, that tipped the scale in convincing the teacher to learn and use the tool for instruction. Within weeks, I was able to co-teach in that classroom and support the educator as they redesigned the lesson to support student success.

Considerations for Team Development

It is key to remember that the purpose of the team is twofold- as the coach, you want to support them directly with intensive coaching experiences and when possible, professional development. You also want to develop their ability to be ambassadors on your campus because that is how you will reach teachers who may not seek out instructional possibilities on their own. That being said, here are some considerations for team development:

The Instructional Ambassadors (or Potential Ambassadors): These are educators who get excited about learning. When they learn something new, they are the first to tell their team and teacher friends. Their passion for honing their craft is infectious, and they are willing to help anyone be successful.

The Positives: I love the positives, I really do. But often the positives are also heavily sought out. They might lead a PLC team, coach, and/or teach multiple preps to three different grades. They may also run two committees each semester—one for teachers and the other for students. My concern with pulling on these school leaders and frankly, true heroes, is that my team could become the "one more thing" that gets dropped from an already-busy schedule.

The Sacrifices: Think *Hunger Games* (Collins, 2009). In that tale, Katniss Everdeen sacrifices herself to save someone else. Often times, you may not get the volunteers you need, and that is okay. Start small. Having someone who feels that they had to "fall on the sword" to save their teacher friends negatively affects the tone of the team. Work with these teachers on an individual basis; be their collaborative partner in hopes that they will demonstrate an interest in the team that is both authentic and beneficial to the needs of the whole team.

The Open Minds*:* When it comes to teaching, this individual is open to change. They don't have to seek out opportunities, but they should be willing to try a new lesson strategy. A teammate with an open mind can share their learning with others in a way that is insightful and engaging.

The Risk-Takers: These folks are strong in their instructional practices, but what makes them even more special is that they never shy away from an opportunity to try something new. Their lessons are fluid, and they understand that adjusting on the fly is a hallmark of creating new experiences for student learning.

As you develop your team, use these archetypes to develop a systematic approach to growing a teacher leader team. This will help you bring a group of people together that are open to working toward the same vision. Moreover, even when each person's motivations to teaching and learning are different, they synergy amongst the group elevates the professional growth experiences for everyone.

Lesson 8: Staying Together—Building a System to Learn, Grow, and Reflect

As a function of our meetings together, we created a process to ensure our time was used effectively. At the start of the year, we began by developing norms and goals. I was really intentional about establishing that both the goals and norms were derived from the group. After the group made these decisions, I used both to help develop future agendas and support our focus during our meetings.

As the year progressed, each meeting began with icebreakers or instructional anticipatory sets. Then we reviewed both our goals and norms to keep us grounded in the purpose of the work. From our goals, we were able to develop action plans. With the ISTE Educator Standards (International Society of Technology Education, 2017) as a foundation, we used our professional development experiences to create an action plan. This ensured that the skills the team was gaining became an integral part of the instructional time. I used Google Classroom to collect these plans each month.

From an instructional coaching perspective, the action plan helped me to support the teacher through co-teaching experi-

> *Go to www.martinembrown.com to access digital content.
>
> Password: 21lessons

ences, establishing or reestablishing our commitments, and helping them use reflective strategies to inform their instruction. Each grading period, we would create a new action plan based on the unique needs of each teacher. I must also add that one of my primary goals during our meetings was to ensure that the action plan was completed before we left for the day, or at least somewhat complete. I built at least 30 minutes into those meetings for that purpose. I also kept the design of the *action plan simple, everything fit on one page, and I never expected the team to write more than a couple of sentences. My goal here is to collect a snapshot of their learning while the information was at the forefront of their mind. It was also important to align this document with ISTE Standards for Educators (International Society of Technology Education, 2017). I was able to ensure that the design of each plan was founded on practices that are based on valid guidelines.

Sample Action Plan

Discuss Your Learning

What have you learned today that you will apply to your current practice? Drop any links or resources that you feel are helpful in this section.

Put it into Action

Decided on a time frame for (specific dates/weeks) implementing your learning. Which lesson or unit are you thinking about using? How can you leverage campus support or your PLC team to aid in implementing this new skill?

Share Your Experience

How will you share your lesson?

Sharing ideas:

- PLC Team/Other teachers observe
- Invite your Instructional Coach to co-teach/observe
- Twitter/social media using our school/district hashtags
- Invite administrators to observe (or depending on the activity join in the lesson)
- Blog, teacher website or student samples

Reflect on The Experience

Using Flipgrid, create a short reflection about your learning.

Lesson 9: Working Together—Co-Teaching and Planning

During my first year as an instructional coach, I made one huge mistake. I failed to make connections and make co-teaching a priority. If teachers sought me out, I did whatever I needed to help and support them. However, I struggled with making those new, initial connections, especially with departments that I had not done much work with before. Remember, I spent a lot of time curating resources, newsletters, and content to support the technology integration on campus. I quickly realized that though the content I provided may have been rich with ideas and resources, most staff did not have time to review it. Furthermore, I hadn't built the kinds of relationships that would support interest in what I was providing. Ironically, I had a leadership team, but I felt that because they were so strong, they did not necessarily need me for co-teaching.

This was the greatest revelation I had during the second year. Not only did the leadership team welcome the idea of co-teaching, but their knowledge, expertise, and openness fostered learning experiences that helped grow my own experiences in co-teaching and instructional coaching with staff who were not on the teacher leadership team. I was now building instructional capacity, and the members of this group were critical to this process.

More Strategies for Teacher Leadership

In my role as an instructional coach, I was given the opportunity to work with fantastic teams over the years. I quickly learned that exploring unique ways to support, encourage, and engage them is key to developing shifts in instructional design. Most teachers just want to know that someone sees them, acknowledges their hard work, and values the commitment that they make each year. There are several ways to do this. Some strategies that I have used are free, while others come with a small investment. Consider the following:

Email and Courtesy Copy Administrators

I know this sounds like common knowledge, but often in the hustle and bustle of moving in and out of classrooms, meetings, and working on projects, we forget to send a short email uplifting the strategies, techniques, or a truly special moment from the learning experience. There are also times when I have asked members of the leadership team to provide professional development. At the end of the presentation, I requested five minutes to complete a survey. I then sent that feedback to the teacher and their supervisors, showcasing their knowledge and expertise as well as how the participants felt about the training.

Write/Co-Write Grants

I have done this several times, and we have won several of the grants we applied for. I have found that often times working with the instructional coach helps the teacher gain confidence in writing their grant. When I have written a grant for a department, I have found that members of the department viewed me as their ally and were more willing to welcome me into their classroom. For example, I co-wrote a grant for a campus 3D Printer. In the weeks after we were awarded the grant, I had three teachers who I had not worked with previously reach out to me to receive training on the device.

Give Exclusive Access

There were times that I had a few apps that needed to be explored before they were released to the whole staff. When I could, I always made sure the leadership team got "first dibs" on these opportunities. If I wanted them to work as teacher leaders in the school, I had to ensure that these were authentic experiences. Providing this type of access gave them the knowledge they needed to help as new tools become available for the campus.

Support Through Your Budget

> *Go to www.martinembrown.com to access digital content.
>
> Password: 21lessons

If your district school provides a budget, consider requesting allocations to support your leadership team. After attending teacher training at the Apple Store, I decided I wanted to replicate that experience for my team. We used that time to complete two different tasks. The first half of the day, we went to the Apple Store* to learn more about the creative tools and applications through products available to the staff. (Apple provides these unique opportunities in their locations for students and teachers. Contact a store near you for more information.) During the second half of the day, we scheduled a time for each teacher to work on their Level 1 Google Certification or Apple Certification. I have said this before--the most invaluable resource a teacher has is time. By requesting funding to have a day for professional learning, the teachers are given the opportunity to practice, reflect, and challenge themselves to discover what's possible in their instruction.

Questions to Consider from Chapter 3:

As a coach, how do you know the instructional coaching/co-teaching experience was successful? How does the teacher know?

Who are critical stakeholders who would show interest in a leadership team?

How will you use the traits listed in this chapter to guide your experiences?

Reflective notes:

4

LESSONS 10-12: LEARNING FROM THE PLN

> *Everyone thinks of changing the world, but no one thinks of changing himself."* — Leo Tolstoy

Teacher Change Is the Toughest Change

When I initially entered education, there was a new trend (at least new to my grade level) called Professional Learning Communities (PLCs). I remember this because it created panic among the team I worked with at the time. This idea of working together, using data to reflect and improve practice, and to do it together seemed otherworldly. It was clear that as a team, we may have chatted about what we were teaching, but everyone was accustomed to having the autonomy to teach whatever they wanted, when they wanted. Even being a novice teacher, I recognized that there was a comfort in using the knowledge and skills I had to teach MY students, in MY classroom. PLCs were essentially the opposite of this philosophy. Here we were, sitting together, nervously looking at one another, wanting to hold on desperately to the way we had always done things. We were unsure if this new strategy would actually help the students we were responsible for.

Of course, PLCs became more of a cornerstone of our planning and instruction, and over time, I tended to lean on them more and more. Much like brick building, we had so much to offer each other, and our conversations, plans, and analysis of the data were key to helping our students reach their full potential. This experience taught me that change knocks at the door of an educator's core instructional belief. This change is the toughest kind to shift. As a fairly new teacher at the time, I remember sensing this process of accepting or rejecting change. However, it wasn't until I was introduced to the concept of Professional Learning Networks (PLNs) that I would truly understand what it means to be uncertain, afraid, or even completely dismissive of new ideas. In acknowledging change, you have to know that there is turbulence that rocks at the core of each of us. Being able to recognize our own resistance to change can help us be more open to its inevitable role in our work.

My Journey into Educational Technology and Professional Learning Networks

During my sixth year as an educator, I was becoming tired and frustrated. My workload was at its peak. I had taught the same lessons, essays, and activities for five years straight. My days of grading pushed well into the evening hours, and many sunny

Sunday afternoons were spent assessing quizzes and tests that were sprawled around my living room floor. I needed a better way to leverage my workday while also gaining some of the precious family time back. Through some training provided by my district and some research on my own, I began to learn about programs like GradeCam and Doceri.

Gradecam essentially gave me more time to focus on improving my instruction. I went from spending two to three hours grading on the weekend to having every student knowing their grade before they left the classroom and having every grade in the grade book before the day ended. Doceri gave me the ability to move about the room during lectures and text analysis. If I had a student(s) who needed the proximity to help them remain focused, I was able to provide it to them. My classroom management improved, my grading became more efficient, and students received feedback much faster. In turn, students responded faster as well. I was starting to breathe again and planned more engaging lessons. I also shared my experiences with my colleagues. My department head asked me to serve as our campus ambassador for technology. In this capacity, I was able to attend training throughout the year that supported using digital tools. It was in this environment that I began to grow and be inspired by a community of educators with an interest in technology.

I Was A Twitter Resistor

It was in these trainings that I was first introduced to growing my PLN through social media platforms like Twitter. I remember this experience specifically because we were participating in a facilitation strategy that required us to move through a series of stations. At each station, the presenter would share information, and we would have time to discuss what we learned and possible classroom implications. When it was my turn to go to the station that discussed Twitter, I had begun to reject the idea before I ever got to my seat. My inner eye roll replaced my usually open and willing-to-learn persona. *Surely, they knew that social media was dangerous?* There had been a slew of new reports about all that can go wrong for educators and social media. I wasn't going to be next, and whatever those teachers were doing online, I was just going to have to miss out. And I did miss out big time.

Lesson 10: Growing your PLC = Growing your PLN

It would be several years before I would begin to explore social media and PLNs as a way to grow my practice. For me, the change occurred from my continued experiences in these trainings and ones similar to them. The conversations I had with educators who engaged in technology in this way sparked my interest and gave me the confidence to navigate in these spaces confidently. In essence, my growth as a member of my local PLC helped to nurture and grow my PLN.

Lesson 11: The PLN Challenges My Thinking

One of the first interactions I had with growing my PLN was participating in Twitter Chats.* PBIS Awards describes Twitter Chats as,

"... conversations that take place on a specific topic on a specific day and at a specific time. Participants in the chat use a #hashtag specific to that topic, which allows for a search to be conducted on the topic even after the chat has ended." (PBIS Awards, n.d.)

> *Go to www.martinembrown.com to access digital content.
>
> Password: 21lessons

One evening, I was excited to participate in a local Twitter chat. I sat on my couch with my phone curled up in my hand. I had searched for the hashtag that evening and waited for the moderators to deliver opening communications and the first question. I learned quickly that the chat followed a specific format. Each new tweet started with a question (Q1, Q2, Q3, etc.), and participants responded using an answer format (A1, A2, A3, etc.). I had never done this before, except for a mock chat during a training where I had learned how to follow a hashtag and how to respond to each question as it was asked. After my first chat, however, I was hooked. I was having conversations about work that I love with others from around the world. These interactions gave me ideas about how I can improve, reminded me of the strategies that were going well, and essentially challenged my thinking. This concept makes me think about my college days. One of the quintessential elements of any pre-service program is the essay you write on educational philosophy. This essay is supposed to outline your vision and beliefs as they relate to your future practice in education. I think if I had to go back and write this document again with all of the knowledge I have gained from my PLN, I would not only have a stronger philosophy, but one that reflects the deep reflective thinking that PLNs and Twitter Chats can reinforce.

Lesson 12: Connect. Connect. Connect.

After overcoming the hardship that comes with change, I recognize that my best professional self can be found in the investment I make in others, and the intellectual investment they make in me. Now more than ever, the need to become better as educators, regardless of our role, is still founded in connection and building relationships with your PLC teams, departments, schools, and the world.

Strategies for Developing your PLN:

Join Twitter. Katrina Stevens (2014) notes that "Out of the 1/2 billion tweets that post every day, 4.2 million are related to education, according to Brett Baker, an account executive at Twitter.com." There is no greater space that one can join that will offer the on-demand professional development that is based on your needs. Use the platform to share the best of your classrooms, schools, and communities and participate in Twitter Chats that help you grow in your practices.

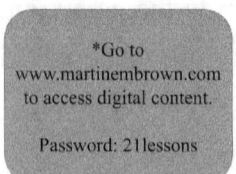

*Go to www.martinembrown.com to access digital content.

Password: 21lessons

One of the most extensive lists of Twitter Chats can found on Education Chats.*

Attend an Edcamp. Edcamps are free professional development conferences that are meant to move away from the traditional conference-

LESSONS 10-12: LEARNING FROM THE PLN

style where the sessions are not created until the participants arrive. Then, based on the needs of the attendees, each room is given specific topics to discuss in which the group shares insights, ideas, tips, and resources. Check out Edcamp.org's* website to learn about events in your area or to start your own.

Join Voxer Groups. Voxer is a walkie talkie app that allows users to create groups and leave voicemail style messages. One huge event held every year is Edcamp Voice.* Similar to a traditional Edcamp, Edcamp Voice uses Voxer to engage in discussions that inform our everyday practices. The EdSquad's* website has an extensive list of Voxer groups that you can join.

Amplify Your Voice: Blog. Vlog. Podcast. I have found blogging and vlogging is a great way to connect with others who share similar ideas or are looking to develop partnerships that support a unified vision for education. Here is a list* of educators who are leaders in the field:

Lizzie Fortin, of Urban Art Room

Lisa Nowakowski and Nancy Minicozzi of TLC Ninja

Katherine Goyette of Wonderexplorelearn.com

Adam Juarez of Tech Coach Juarez

Kim Cofino and Clint Hamada of #coachbetter Podcast

Claudio Zavala of I am Claudius

Nicole Turner of Educator's Caravan

Shawn McCusker & Greg Kulowiec of So We've Been Thinking

Jeff Bradbury and Nicholas Amaral of Ask the Tech Coach

Kimberly Mattina of The Suite Talk

Penny Christensen of the Hot Lunch Tray

Kasey Bell of Shake Up Learning

Attend Local, State, & National Conferences and Connect. Often times, we attend conferences to collect information, learn, and bring said information back to our campuses. This is also a time to make connections that build professional bridges that support student and adult learning.

Questions to Consider from Chapter 4:

How do you engage with other educators outside of your local community?

In what ways will you expand your professional reach to support your professional learning communities?

Reflective notes:

LESSON 13-15: BACK TO THE NOT-SO-BASICS OF SCHOOL

 *Knowledge is Power."* —Frederick Douglass

"You Know What? I'm Done."

I had spent the past four years shifting between enjoying my time as an undergrad while also keeping a sharp beeline on my goal. I had just graduated from college. As I held my bachelor's degree in one hand and newly-stamped teaching certificate in the other, I concluded that school was behind me. Yes, I knew that I *could* continue my education and head to graduate school. As a matter of fact, I am sure that it was suggested to me on more than one occasion. I was single, unmarried, and had the time to continue my studies in isolation or even manage both as began my search for my first teaching job. But here is the truth: **I. Was. Done.** I desperately wanted to be on the other side of the desk and had no plans on putting myself back on the other side in a formal sense. In retrospect, at least for my journey, it was probably a good thing that I was able to apply the same tenacity that I had for school into my classroom. You see, I didn't ever plan on furthering my education. I had what I needed to do what I was passionate about, and I was ready to make a difference in the lives of students every day. The more I think about it, this steadfastness, albeit stubbornness, put me on a road of constant professional development as I grew in my practice. However, going back to school and extending your education (both informally and formally) supports your ability to hone your craft, and to enhance your perception on your daily work and its connections to leadership, school law/policy, and research.

Maybe I Am NOT "So Done"

My 10th year as an educator came to an end, and as I transitioned into my role as an instructional coach, it was clear that I needed more training. I also have to add that the digital leadership team in my district played a huge role and fostering that spark for a renewed desire for formal education. The instructional technology meetings I had been attending the past couple of years had done an excellent job of consistently staying ahead of the curve- not only with emerging technologies, but also pedagogical principles that help to support the instructional uses of tools and learning strategies. They pushed me to redesign my lessons and pose new questions that I had not considered before. It is from this place that I began to consider continuing my education. I had several areas that I wanted to explore, but the key element I wanted to gain from the pursuit of my master's degree was more knowledge as it relates to instructional design and leadership.

No More Brick & Mortar Learning

As a college student, I was as traditional as one gets in modern-day higher education. We had computer labs in all the dorms, we had online access to research tools and our newly renovated library. For the most part, all of the instructions were directly given by the professor. I typed my assignments and printed them out, and my college portal was used primarily to check grades and email. The final semester of my senior year, the school was offering the first of their online classes. Students would meet once at the beginning of the semester and again at the end of the semester for attendance purposes, but the rest of the learning would be completed online. I signed up for the course, explored the online content, and within three weeks, I dropped it. To be honest, I just didn't think I could be successful as an online learner and with graduation quickly approaching. I figured that my formal education was ending and the "online classes" concept would be left to my former classmates to figure out.

Then I got married.

Then I had kids.

Then I realized I wanted to go back to school, and the best way to do that was in an online program. Go figure.

The truth was that after ten years as an educator, I indeed was a different learner. I can't say enough that I have worked in a district that is constantly evolving both in technology and in pedagogy. This allowed me to begin, at least from a teaching perspective, to visit the concept of online learning through the instructional platforms they provided. With this realization, I dusted off my laptop keys and enrolled in an online master's Program.

Lesson 13: Speak Up! (From Your Computer)

One of the most valuable aspects of the online coursework I experienced were the discussion forums. Discussion forums are threads that replicate classroom engagement among peers and the professor throughout the class. Each week, the professor would pose a question(s), and we were responsible for responding to questions, as well as to one another's responses. I found this mode of communicating and learning so powerful because, for the first time in my career, I was able to have deep, thoughtful discussions with people from all over the country and from a diverse set of educational roles. Their viewpoints helped me think (and rethink) about mine. When we had forums that required us to submit work and then provide and receive feedback, it was an excellent opportunity to gauge the effectiveness of our products as well as to examine how our classmates interpreted what we were learning. When enrolling in these courses, you have two choices: do the bare minimum to get through the coursework, or to authentically engaging in these discussions. Engaging in the latter of the two is the only way to improve your instructional and digital leadership.

Lesson 14: Blending Leadership and Technical Skills

Often, I am asked to review resumes for positions that are not instructional. I have examined many resumes from aspiring instructional coaches, facilitators, and assistant principals. The first segment of feedback that I always give immediately is regarding quality and/or presence of leadership skills as they are communicated throughout the resume. However, I think that my recommitment to continue my education helped to bolster this feedback. Going back to school allowed me to broaden my views outside of the classroom. Previously, I had a microscopic view of teaching and learning, peering down on my students, in my subject, at my school. My coursework gave me the opportunity to understand how to effectively lead better, while also blending in the technical skills that I was learning into those experiences. What I specifically thought was unique about my journey was the growth of my technical skills and how those skills supported my ability to help build processes, systems, and design elements for school and district initiatives.

Furthermore, my projects helped me to engage with my school in ways that I had not previously considered. I hosted professional development, performed focus groups, and lead committees- all of which allowed me to model technology use while building my leadership skills. As you consider the value of continuing your education, know that good curriculum should always help you grow in your professional role. If you aren't stepping out of your comfort zone (especially if you are teaching simultaneously), then you are not setting yourself up to empower others as an instructional leader.

Lesson 15: Learning NEVER Stops.

What if you can't go back to school? Below are several examples of strategies you can use to ensure that regardless of whether going back to school is within your reach or not, you can continue to remain an empowered educator:

Volunteer for School and District Initiatives. Some of the most meaningful learning you can get comes from what your district provides. Contact campus and district leadership and see what is available to you. What I like about these programs is that they are often built with standards and district goals at the core of the planning. You can ensure that you are learning and that what you take back to your classroom or coaching experience is on target with those goals.

Sign up for Professional Development. Many districts and educational agencies offer free or low-cost (cheaper than tuition) classes. Talk to both campus and district administrators or write grants to see if funding is available for out-of-district training.

Get Certified. This is another low-cost way to ensure you are constantly growing. G-Suite for Education* offers a leveled certification process that relates to their products and their correlation to instruction and learning. If you have an idea that you want to bring to fruition, they also have a Google Innovators program in which accepted applicants receive high-quality, in-depth training to help them grow their concept.

Apple also has its own certification program called Apple

> *Go to
> www.martinembrown.com
> to access digital content.
>
> Password: 21lessons

Teacher*, and if you apply to become an Apple Distinguished Educator, selected candidates also participate in a three-day program to develop their ideas. Consider your areas of interest to determine if there are certification programs available to extend and deepen your knowledge.

State & National Organization Programming. Check state and national organizations for online programs. With membership, some of the programs are free or at a fraction of the cost of traditional and online courses.

Who knew I would go back to school? I certainly would never have thought that I would earn my Masters, but here I am several years out, and I won't lie--I crave the classroom once again. I have become more creative in my journey and actively avoid complacency within my own professional development. As you reflect on continuing your education, choose a learning path that is best for you, but never stop learning.

> **Questions to Consider from Chapter 5:**
>
> In what ways will you use your education to leverage professional growth?
>
> What are some avenues you can take to become actively involved in your educational growth?

Reflective notes:

LESSON 16-18: HOWDY PARTNER! INSTRUCTIONAL COACHING PARTNERSHIPS

> *If you want to go fast, go alone. If you want to go far, go together."* —African Proverb

Lesson 16: Critical Collaborations: Librarian-Coach PLCs

*Go to www.martinembrown.com to access digital content.

Password: 21lessons

When examining the instructional support in schools, there is nothing more powerful than the combined efforts of the instructional coach and librarian. I began working with my campus librarians after earning a grant that provided the campus with 25 Breakout EDU Boxes.* These kits are essentially compartments that have five or six different locks on them. Teachers can design lessons and activities in which students go through a series of clues to unlock the box. This gamified approach to learning engages students through communication, collaboration, critical thinking, and creativity. At the time, I lacked the resources and space to house and check out the boxes, and the librarians were willing to make the boxes a part of their instructional resources. What I didn't realize is that this was only just the beginning. From those experiences, I learned several lessons regarding collaborating with campus librarians:

Think. Grow. Build. Together. While not all of your projects will be done together, engage in think tanks or brainstorming sessions. As instructional support learning communities, members bring ideas to the table to capture various perspectives. These think tanks helped the team craft phenomenal lessons or co-teaching opportunities.

Acknowledged Discourse. Create environments where discourse is welcomed. You shouldn't always agree when planning and designing lessons or programming. Some of your best ideas will derive from discourse. When working together and an idea is challenged, that could mean that it is truly special. Finding a way to nurture the best concepts is key to ensuring that teachers desire to integrate the resources throughout the school year.

Streamline Planning. Explore ways to embed district, campus, and library-related planning into your project to ensure that teacher-coach connections and librarian-teacher connections are present. Create partnerships that embrace co-planning activities to meet the needs of both the librarian and the coach. The key for us was to ensure the library was seen as a space from which all content areas could benefit, and that when a teacher was considering projects and activities for their students, they had the support of both the instructional coach and librarian in their corner.

Lesson 17: Support Administrators Through Systems

As we move into establishing future-ready digital competencies in schools, supporting administrators will foster shifts in thinking campus-wide. One way to do this is to help develop systems. Are there systems on your campus that are a bit archaic? Time-consuming? Or use a lot of resources? Seek out opportunities to help streamline these processes. As the instructional coach, meet with each administrator and brainstorm ways to transition the systems into digital processes. Research and use tools such as Google Forms and Google Sites to develop digital versions of the process. Working on these projects will hone your skills with tools that impact the entire building. More importantly, your collaborations with administrators will help teachers see the value of using the tools, and they will follow up with you regarding how to scale similar systems for their classrooms.

Lesson 18: Collaborate for Community Partnerships

Fostering change at your school means becoming a community stakeholder as well. For the past couple of years, I have been working with other instructional coaches, librarians, and educators on community-related projects. One of the first projects that I worked on was starting a community Edcamp. As a team of instructional coaches, we wanted to embed the spirit of Edcamp in our local community and established several local Edcamps.

One of my favorite Edcamp experiences was Edcamp Change. What made this Edcamp special is that we decided to invite students to come to the event. We were unsure how teachers or students were going to react to the experience, but the end result was more than I could have ever hoped for. The students were able to offer advice to one another regarding college and postsecondary plans in some sessions. In other sessions, teachers asked students about current trends in their learning and wanted to know more about how educators can better serve their needs. I was taken aback by the willingness of teachers and students to ensure that everyone left the Edcamp with more insight on how to work together better to ensure student success. Nourishing these types of partnerships is what will help to redefine campus culture and support the ongoing learning of educators and students.

> **Questions to Consider from Chapter 6:**
>
> How do you currently engage with campus stakeholders to ensure that you build impactful coaching relationships?
>
> When considering your administration, how will you promote new systems to meet the needs of campus structures?
>
> How have you connected with your librarians? In what ways will you grow this dynamic to help meet your unique goals?

Reflective notes:

7

LESSON 19-21: NOT ANOTHER PD?

> *You cannot dream yourself into a character; you must hammer and forge yourself one."* —Henry David Thoreau

Of all the areas of instructional coaching, providing professional development has been one of the most terrifying and rewarding experiences. During my journey of becoming a coach, leading adult learners was integrated into my role as the campus ambassador for technology integration. I worked with a team of colleagues to develop engaging training founded in the ISTE Standards for technology integration (ISTE, 2017).

I knew right away that I wanted to be different. For years I attended trainings that lacked what I needed as a learner. Death by PowerPoint was rampant, and it was often hard to see a connection between the information being shared and the work I did with students every day. As I think about my transformation from teacher to coach-teacher, I realized that my district leaders and trainers were critical in my transformation from teacher to teacher leader to a teaching coach. The strongest of them taught me that professional development should mirror instruction. Adult learners are most engaged when they can use at least one, if not more, strategies, tools, techniques, etc. within a couple of days of being introduced to them. My years in education have also taught me that canned, disorganized, or chaotic professional development creates disengaged educators who return to their schools and classrooms resolute in their belief that professional development cannot help them with the day to day practice of teaching and learning.

Lesson 19: Risk = Rewarding PD Experiences

I am in a constant search for ideas that will make the professional development that I provide feel unique and special. This process of trying out concepts comes with a substantial risk. The truth is that as much as teachers say they hate presentation, lecture-style, "growth" sessions, many do find a sense of comfort in that layout. Much like our students, it is easy to become disengaged when the training is structurally ineffective. Previous experiences with lackluster professional development sessions and lack of actionable goal setting related to professional growth are key factors that bred distracted adult learners. Some colleagues arrive at professional development with their stack of papers needing to be graded—more recently, their email program is pulled up, and they are ready to wrap up the correspondences that they haven't had a chance to get to. Even the chatty teacher may have just realized their longtime edu-buddy is sitting at their table and is more than excited to catch up with an old friend than participate in training.

To be honest, I get it—if someone is going to stand in front of me with a clicker and paraphrase from a really big index card, I would take that time to do some multitasking, grab a copy of the presentation, and do more research later. I live for these moments, because it is then that I take many risks to earn the attention of my colleagues; to provide them with an experience that will captivate and have them consider what they can do to enhance their instruction today- not the "maybe in the summer" ideal that ravages promising professional growth. Below are several risks I've taken that have helped to win over adult learners.

You've Got to Move it, Move it. At conferences, especially large conferences, I meet everyone at the door, or I go to the tables and say hello. If time permits, I will learn a little bit about where they are from, and I never begin from the podium. Ever. You have to consider that conference attendees will see traditional "sage on the stage" style introductions over and over again within the course of a three- to five-day conference. By beginning the session from the floor with your audience, you are more likely to reset your participants' expectations of the session.

Call and Response. Begin your session with a call and response. I love to start with, "When I SAY 'TECH!' you SAY 'READY!'" I am careful not to overdo it as participants will grow tired fast, but as a start, this usually gets everyone's attention and gets everyone on the same page as we begin our learning journey. Keep in mind here that this is all about personality. If you know that calls and responses are atypical for your communication style, choose something that works for you. I have also seen people ask for cheers based on number of years in education, geographic location, or college preference. All of these strategies are ways to gain your participants' attention quickly without making them feel forced.

Lesson 20: Plan Unicorn-Style PD

One of the reasons why I love professional development is that it is an opportunity to be different. My philosophy is that all participants should experience learning in a way that is new to them. I will often examine a conference or district training offerings and begin with two major purposes in mind. My first mission is the purpose- what do I want the participants to learn? The second goal is to communicate those thoughts and ideas in a way that is not only out-of-the-box, but it blows the box out of the atmosphere.

PD Play Time

In the classroom, many students learn by doing, and the same is true for adult learners as well. Whenever possible, I design professional development sessions that focus on how students will experience the instructional strategy. Performing digital breakouts with adult learners is a great way to activate engaging professional learning. They are similar to the Breakout Edu physical boxes, which feature locks with a series of clues for students to "break" or open, but in a digital breakout, all of them use a Google Form or Google Sites. In the past, I would share this instructional strategy with colleagues, highlighting the power of student engagement and team building that is developed through this breakout. Teachers were excited, but struggled to conceptualize how the activity would be performed in the classroom. During the next round of professional development I provided, I decided to create a digital breakout that would take approximately 40 minutes to complete. Digital breakouts provide the space to perform authentic learning that is based on critical thinking, collaboration, communication, and creativity. Putting educators back in the seat of the authentic learner aids them in having a clear picture of how a lesson can be modified to meet the needs of their students. No slide presentation can ever do that.

As I moved around the room, the teachers were committed to unlocking the clues. They were stumped on other clues and cheered or high-fived each other as they cracked the codes and overcame obstacles. As participants left, they thanked me for opening their eyes to a new strategy. They wanted more time to learn how to create their own breakouts for their students, and they mentioned that the session gave them a huge reprieve from a morning of sit and get presenters.

When I reviewed my feedback, it was clear that teachers wanted a longer session (a rare request) or to have this session double blocked so that they can learn the backend of the digital breakout development after the initial activity. As a presenter, this is a huge win because it lets me know that the content provided engagement that made teachers want to learn more. Most importantly, that spark that happened in professional development lit a fire in several of the teachers who immediately began to research and create their own digital breakouts for their classrooms. Unicorn-style PD is centered around designing concepts with activities that are challenging enough for adult learners while also leveraging its accessibility for various grade levels.

Lesson 21: Prioritize and Analyze Feedback

Early on in my path of providing training and development, I needed feedback. In my local professional community, my colleagues always gave me the thumbs up and support. I knew my work family supported the work I did and were appreciative of what I had to offer them. But as I began to engage in more professional development experiences locally, regionally, and nationally, I desired to ensure that every person in the room walked away with at least one nugget of knowledge to take back to their campuses. Feedback became critical in helping me to provide the learning experiences possible for the educators I interacted with.

Yikes. That Didn't Go So Well.

Not every professional development session will be successful. At a regional conference, I had planned what I thought was a solid session regarding tips and strategies for instructional coaches. I had my transitions thought out. I had practiced my anecdotes; my Google Forms and links had been checked and worked. There was just one problem: as soon as the room of 150 people began to log in and prep for my session, every ounce of Wi-Fi slowed to a turtle's space, and I couldn't even get my slide deck to work. I spent what seemed like an hour (it was probably six to eight minutes) trying to move forward and recover. Several people walked out, and I perceived that they felt I was incompetent and lacked the skills to communicate my message. (This is probably not true, as even I have left a session to take care of business or meet with a colleague.) I slowed my pace, took a deep breath, and pressed forward. The feedback was mixed, some felt the session was good but lacked the "how-to" format that they hoped for. Others applauded my ability to overcome the technology issues. Others pointed out errors that I had made that I hadn't noticed. It was then that I realized the feedback (especially if provided anonymously) can be used to help me deliver better content at the next event. For this reason, I have a mix of strategies I use to collect feedback and have found it to be a powerful tool in designing content for adult learners.

Create Short Surveys. I have reduced my feedback form to no more than two or three questions, with one of those questions being a comment. Long surveys are rarely completed with authenticity and are less likely to have comments. Also, I always devote the last six minutes of any session to completing the survey. This has helped me gain more responses. I often combine this with a Q&A session. Participants will likely stick around for this section and will complete the feedback form while they listen or wait to have their questions answered.

Social Media Feedback. Throughout my presentation, I make sure to ask participants to tag me and Tweet out anything they felt was meaningful. I do this for two reasons. First, I use that feedback to better understand what content resonated with the group and make notes to continue to emphasize those concepts in future sessions. Secondly, when the feedback is detailed, I will contact the person and request permission to embed the tweet in my digital portfolio. When sharing my body of work with others, I now have a systematic way of communicating how educators connect with the content I provide.

*Go to www.martinembrown.com to access digital content.

Password: 21lessons

Give & Get Feedback. In place of simply a copy providing the presentation, ask participants to fill out a form and use mail merge programs like Formule* or Autocrat* to automatically send an email to participants after they have submitted the form.

Questions to Consider from Chapter 7:

How can you ensure that you create "out of the box" experiences for your colleagues?

In what ways do you capitalize on the feedback provided when you facilitate professional development?

What strategies have you used in the classroom that can be modeled during professional development sessions?

Reflective notes:

8

CONCLUSION

During my second year of teaching, I had the awesome opportunity to be mentored by a veteran teacher. Her name was Judy, and she totally changed how I viewed instruction. At the time, I was teaching English and had a classroom of students who refused to speak. The silence was deafening. No matter what I said, the students just sat there. They read and did the work as I asked, but they refused to interact with me or each other. I went to Judy for help and shared with her that I thought that their unwillingness to engage was uncommon, and I could not figure out how to change this dynamic. As always, Judy was more than willing to come by and observe my classroom. The feedback she provided altered my perception of that class and how I taught students going forward. She noted that the students appeared to be afraid to speak up, this fear had less to do with my teaching and more to do with potentially responding to content incorrectly and being viewed as academically inadequate. Judy gave me strategies and resources to help my students grow their confidence. She shared her expertise as it relates to building relationships with reluctant classes and supported me as I built a plan for creating a safe instructional environment. As the year progressed, my ability to engage the class improved, and I learned to adjust my strategies to meet the needs of each class period. I shudder to think what would have happened if I didn't have Judy to help me better understand myself and my students. The truth was, Judy was a kind and loving teacher, but she was also the coach I needed. Her instructional strategies were founded in research-based practices and 30 years of experience. She made everyone, students and colleagues alike, feel valued and important. She made time to listen and was always willing to help me explore ideas, observe my class, and offer feedback. Her insights were invaluable and shifted my educational and instructional lens. Though she was not an instructional coach in title, this master teacher fostered the core of my beliefs as it relates to supporting colleagues. When I look back on her impact on my development as an educator, Judy's ability to see more in me than I saw in myself became the catalyst for my own growth. As an instructional coach, especially when your role is associated with technology, know that you will have challenges, but at the foundation of your work is the desire to see the best in people. Your commitment to this belief, along with consistent growth and practice in developing your skills, will be at the heart of your ability to positively influence those around you. For those of you that are new to coaching, I hope that you can take these lessons and use them as pathways to guide your practice. Much like a carpenter, it takes a myriad of tools to shape one's coaching

CONCLUSION

experience. My sincerest goal is that experienced coaches will be able to take these ideas and tips and add them to their own instructional coaching toolbox. The fluidity that is derived from a strong coaching partnership never truly ends. If anything, it grows and expands because successful coaches, schools, and teachers are invested in the process. The impact of putting student learning at the center of the work we do every day provides eternal hope for a brighter future.

A Summary of the Lessons

Lesson 1: Expand Your Reach—What is your Why?

Knowing who is as an instructional coach is key to understanding your impact. You can't influence your stakeholders without having a strong foundation in your purpose.

Lesson 2: "When I Was in The Classroom" Myth

Having clarity about your role helps you remain a teaching partner, and you avoid becoming the sage with no stage. Your memories of your teaching and learning rarely support what teachers need the most, someone to listen and help them navigate their ideas.

Lesson 3: Become A Partner and Researcher

You are time on its feet. Use that time to speed up the process of innovation in classrooms. Using part of the workday to maximize teacher resources is essential to ensuring that grand ideas and strategies become learning realities.

Lesson 4: A Vision of Hope

Believing in people and their desire to bring the best of themselves is the cornerstone of instructional coaching. With this hope, you can embrace everyone and remain a positive influence on those around you.

Lesson 5: *EARS* Wide Open

When you want to get to the core of teacher needs, there is no other tool more powerful than your ears. Your ability to listen will help you develop long term coaching relationships that will increase the growth of those you support.

Lesson 6: Heart for Coaching—Language

Not just any word, but every word is significant. Analysis and reflection of how what you say and how you communicate those ideas are critical to sustaining coaching conversations.

Lesson 7: Coming Together—Developing Your Team

Creating a team provides an outlet to work with teachers who are willing and are doing great work. As their partner, the work you do with them is often shared with others, and that influence is critical to building instructional capacity in schools.

Lesson 8: Staying Together—Building A System to Learn, Grow, And Reflect

Working with your team is about how you collaborate in meetings to guarantee that everyone's professional growth needs are being met. An action plan can help solidify that commitment to growth, and it should be completed or at least mostly completed during the meeting.

Lesson 9: Working Together—Co-Teaching and Planning

Meeting with a team of teacher leaders committed to professional growth will help you establish opportunities to co-teach. This is the time to connect and grow with teachers and learners, and to engage in coaching cycles with educators who are on your team.

Lesson 10: Growing your PLC = Growing Your PLN

Engaging with colleagues locally who have a PLN is a good start to growing your own. As an instructional coach, it is important to note that you will also become a model for others as well.

Lesson 11: The PLN Challenges My Thinking

Participating in Twitter Chats will help you explore your ideas and those of others across the globe.

Lesson 12: Connect. Connect. Connect.

To give and get the most from your PLN, know that these relationships can flourish online and face to face. Use a variety of techniques to ensure you are building connections and not just a network.

Lesson 13: Speak Up! (From Your Computer)

Use the discussion forums in your studies as a place to pose questions and engage in conversations often based on research and the curriculum. You lose out on an opportunity to truly grow when your participation is minimal.

Lesson 14: Blending Leadership and Technical Skills

The assignments and projects you work on during your coursework can expand your skill and reconsider school processes. Take full advantage of this opportunity to explore new tools, devices, and platforms.

Lesson 15: Learning NEVER Stops.

It's as simple as that. Formally or informally continuing your education is key to creating engaging learning environments for students that are based on current research and digital/instructional standards.

Lesson 16: Critical Collaborations: Librarian-Coach PLCs

Working with librarians and media specialists will establish your own teaching support PLCs that are centered around helping teachers improve teaching practices while also using library resources/knowledge base to foster the growth.

Lesson 17: Support Administrators Through Systems

Pairing up with administrators to review, analyze and build digital systems to enhance schoolwide processes models best practices for technology integration. Help your leaders establish themselves as digital leaders.

Lesson 18: Collaborate for Community Partnerships

Examine your community's needs and collaborate with colleagues to build events that are centered around teaching, learning, and student growth.

Lesson 19: Risk = Rewarding PD Experiences

Reject the norm as it relates to training; take strategic risks in the techniques you use to deliver content. Your participants will be more open to valuing what you have to share.

Lesson 20: Plan Unicorn-Style PD

Consider ways that the PD can reflect out of the box thinking.

Any training that includes research-based facilitation strategies or simulations will provide participants with new ways to engage in their learning.

Lesson 21: Prioritize and Analyze Feedback

Organize training so that you always give time for your audience to provide feedback. Make sure you review the data you receive and adjust your sessions so that all participants get the best you have to offer.

ACKNOWLEDGMENTS

There would be no words without a team of mentors, colleagues, friends, and family who have allowed me to be a part of their journey. I would first like to thank Denisha Macon of Macon Designs; you made my vision for this book a reality. To the EduMatch Family and EduMatch Publishing, thank you for giving me this opportunity and for providing structures to aid in this publication. To Sarah, thank you for seeing me as a writer well before I saw that in myself. I am an author. (Look, I said it. LOL.) You helped me get there. Knikole, I knew our educator spirits were linked from the first time I met you. Thank you for your willingness to be a part of this book and for always allowing me to be my best self with you. To Brian, Angie, Bonnie, Nelson, Kathy, Judy, April, Ansil, Shondreka, Adrian, Tyra, Jason, Marquis, Cheynne, Jason T., Elissa, and Carole Jane, thank you for pushing me to be the best teacher, educator, instructional coach, and author I can be. To my Educator BAEs,

Shaneia, Tanika, Alice, Danielle, Elizabeth, Sandra, Rhonda, and Ayasha, your support, love, and the ability to lift one another's crown are what makes each of you a Queen, and I am blessed to be able to know each of you. To my lifelong friend, Jannell, you listen, and then you listen some more…then you bring me back to my senses. I am so lucky to have you and your encouragement. To my siblings, Donald and Jasmine, you guys have been my reading partners and my inspiration, know that I love you dearly and appreciate your support. Though my father Donald is gone, I must say thank you for running alongside me, and having my back--I know you would be proud. To my mother, Jennifer, you are the foundation and the ultimate coach. You have always known that I could do anything, and you made sure you prepared me for this moment, thank you for loving hard and unconditionally. To my children, Devin, Maxwell, and Charlotte, you are what gives me hope for a better tomorrow. I thank you for reminding me that children are at the center of a better future. Most of all, I want to thank my husband Kevin, your ability to shake me from the page with your love, kindness, and laughter is what makes me excited to wake up to you each day. None of this could have happened without you, and I am forever thankful.

REFERENCES

Aguilar, E. (2013). The art of coaching: effective strategies for school transformation. *San Francisco: Jossey-Bass, A Wiley Brand.*

Collins, S. (2009). The Hunger Games. *London: Scholastic.*

Kee, K., Anderson, K., Dearning, V., Harris, E., & Shuster, F. (2010). Results coaching: The new essential for school leaders. *Thousand Oaks, CA: Corwin Press.*

Kee, K., Anderson, K., Dearing, V., & Shuster, F. (2017). RESULTS coaching next steps: Leading for growth and change. *Thousand Oaks, CA: Corwin A SAGE Company. Pgs. 58-59*

REFERENCES

ISTE Standards for Educators. (2017). Retrieved from https://www.iste.org/standards/for-educators

Knight, J. (2015, October 19). *The Power of Words.* Retrieved from https://www.instructionalcoaching.com/power-words/

Knight, J. (2018). *The impact cycle: What instructional coaches should do to foster powerful improvements in teaching.* Thousand Oaks, CA: Corwin, A Sage Company.

Kraft, M. A., & Blazar, D. (2018, March 12). *Taking Teacher Coaching to Scale: Can Personalized Training Become Standard Practice?* Retrieved from https://www.educationnext.org/taking-teacher-coaching-to-scale-can-personalized-training-become-standard-practice/

Stanier, M. B. (2016). *The Coaching Habit: Say Less, Ask More & Change the Way You Lead Forever.* Retrieved from https://boxofcrayons.com/the-coaching-habit-book/

Stevens, K. (2014, April 30). *Twitter Exec Reports that Educators Dominate the Twitter-sphere - EdSurge News.* Retrieved from https://www.edsurge.com/news/2014-04-30-twitter-exec-reports-that-educators-dominate-the-twitter-sphere

Trach, S. (2014, November/December). Inspired Instructional Coaching. Retrieved from https://www.naesp.org/sites/default/files/Trach_ND14.pdf

Will, M. (2019, July 31). Instructional Coaching Works, Says a New Analysis. But There's a Catch. Retrieved from http://blogs.edweek.org/edweek/teacherbeat/2018/07/instructional_coaching_works_research.html

APPENDIX

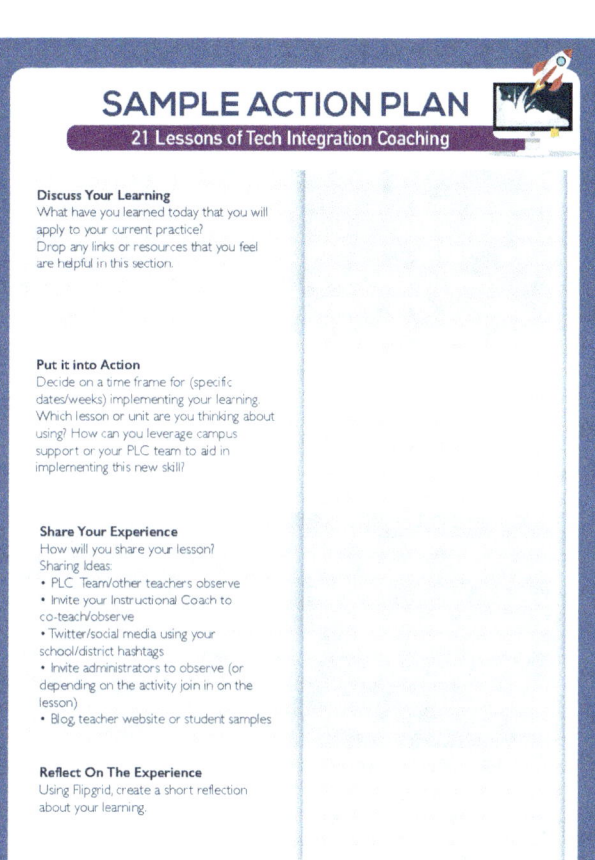

SAMPLE ACTION PLAN
21 Lessons of Tech Integration Coaching

Discuss Your Learning
What have you learned today that you will apply to your current practice?
Drop any links or resources that you feel are helpful in this section.

Put it into Action
Decide on a time frame for (specific dates/weeks) implementing your learning. Which lesson or unit are you thinking about using? How can you leverage campus support or your PLC team to aid in implementing this new skill?

Share Your Experience
How will you share your lesson?
Sharing Ideas:
- PLC Team/other teachers observe
- Invite your Instructional Coach to co-teach/observe
- Twitter/social media using your school/district hashtags
- Invite administrators to observe (or depending on the activity join in on the lesson)
- Blog, teacher website or student samples

Reflect On The Experience
Using Flipgrid, create a short reflection about your learning.

Appendix A. Sample Action Plan

WEBSITES

Apple Store Field Trip (For Students & Teachers)
https://www.apple.com/retail/fieldtrip/

10 Twitter Chats for Educators
https://www.pbisrewards.com/blog/twitter-chats-educators/

Edcamp Voice
https://www.edcampvoice.com/

Education Chats
https://sites.google.com/site/twittereducationchats/education-chat-official-list

Edcamp Foundation
https://www.edcamp.org/

Edsquad
http://www.theedsquad.org/voxer

G-Suite for Education Certification
https://teachercenter.withgoogle.com/certification

Apple Teacher Certification
https://www.apple.com/education/apple-teacher/

Breakout Edu
https://www.breakoutedu.com/

Formule
https://chrome.google.com/webstore/detail/form-mule-email-merge-uti/kabhamaiihmaphgpijdolgcihofefajn?utm_source=permalink

Autocrat
https://chrome.google.com/webstore/detail/autocrat/ppgnklghfnlijoafjjkpoakpjjpdkgdj?utm_source=permalink

COACHES TO FOLLOW

Lizzie Fortin, of Urban Art Room

Lisa Nowakowski and Nancy Minicozzi of TLC Ninja

Katherine Goyette of Wonderexplorelearn.com

Adam Juarez of Tech Coach Juarez Kim Cofino and Clint Hamada of Eduro Learning

Claudio Zavala of I am Claudius

Nicole Turner of Educator's Caravan

Shawn McCusker & Greg Kulowiec of So We've Been Thinking

Jeff Bradbury and Nicholas Amaral of Ask the Tech Coach

Kimberly Mattina of The Suite Talk

Penny Christensen of the Hot Lunch Tray

Kasey Bell of Shake Up Learning

OTHER EDUMATCH TITLES

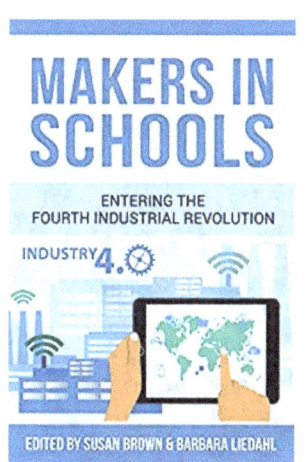

Makers in Schools
Editors: Susan Brown & Barbara Liedahl
The maker mindset sets the stage for the Fourth Industrial Revolution, empowering educators to guide their students.

Divergent EDU by Mandy Froehlich
The concept of being innovative can be made to sound so simple. But what if the development of the innovative thinking isn't the only roadblock?

EduMatch Snapshot in Education (2018)
EduMatch® is back for our third annual Snapshot in Education.

OTHER EDUMATCH TITLES

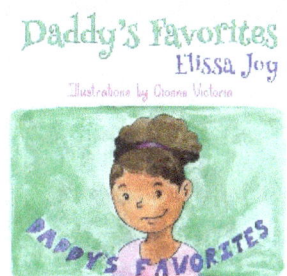

Daddy's Favorites by Elissa Joy
Illustrated by Dionne Victoria
Five-year-old Jill wants to be the center of everyone's world. But, her most favorite person in the world, without fail, is her Daddy.

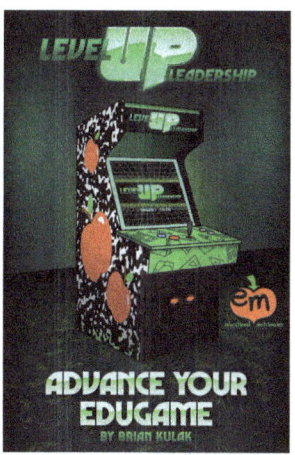

Level Up Leadership by Brian Kulak
Gaming has captivated its players for generations and cemented itself as a fundamental part of our culture. In order to reach the end of the game, they all need to level up.

The Edupreneur by Dr. Will
The Edupreneur is a 2019 documentary film that takes you on a journey into the successes and challenges of some of the most recognized names in K-12 education consulting.

In Other Words by Rachelle Dene Poth
In Other Words is a book full of inspirational and thought-

provoking quotes that have pushed the author's thinking and inspired her.

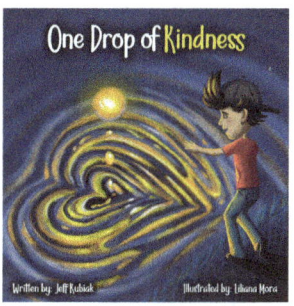

One Drop of Kindness by Jeff Kubiak
This children's book, along with each of you, will change our world as we know it. It only takes *One Drop of Kindness to fill a heart with love.*

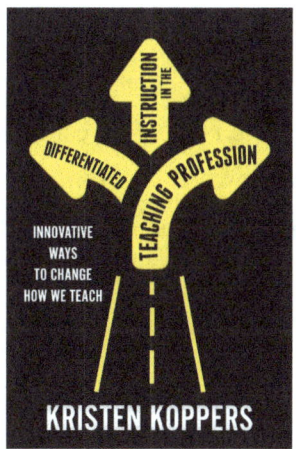

Differentiated Instruction in the Teaching Profession by Kristen Koppers

Differentiated Instruction in the Teaching Profession is an innovative way to use critical thinking skills to create strategies to help all students succeed. This book is for educators of all levels who want to take the next step into differentiating their instruction.

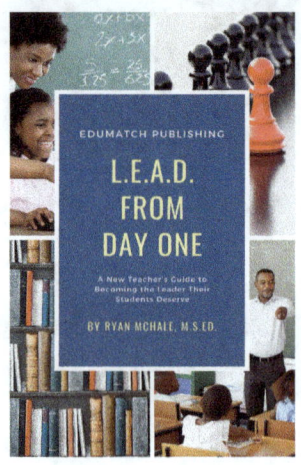

L.E.A.D. from Day One by Ryan McHale

L.E.A.D. from Day One is a go-to resource to help educators outline a future plan toward becoming a teacher leader. The purpose of this book is to help you see just how easily you can transform your entire mindset to become the leader your students need you to be. So what are you waiting for? The time is now.

www.ingramcontent.com/pod-product-compliance
Lightning Source LLC
Chambersburg PA
CBHW071250070526
44583CB00017B/2403